The Meaning of Our Faith

Religious Poetry

by

Rev. Ernest L. Hamlin

DORRANCE PUBLISHING CO
EST. 1920
PITTSBURGH, PENNSYLVANIA 15238

Dorrance Publishing Co
585 Alpha Drive
Pittsburgh, PA 15238
Visit our website at *www.dorrancebookstore.com*

ISBN: 979-8-89341-440-0
eISBN: 979-8-89341-939-9

Table of Contents

Without God, There Is No Way!

Adam and Eve stood naked one day
From righteousness they had strayed away
They ate the forbidden fruit that day
And without God, there is no way!

The Israelites were without God
They stood trembling on earth's dusty sod
It was indeed a sad moment in their day
For without God, there is no way!

King Belshazzar made merry one day
All of a sudden he didn't know what to say
For King Belshazzar found out that day
Without God, there is no way!

Ananias and Sapphira only a portion did they give
And this is the reason they ceased to live
The hand of God moved that day
And without God, there is no way!

Judas, one of the twelve, sold his soul
For thirty pieces of silver, so I'm told
Judas had to find out the hard way
I know without God, there is no way!

Peter thought he was faithful in every way,
But he denied Christ thrice in one day
Peter wept bitterly, I must say—
Because without God, there is no way!

Rev. Ernest L. Hamlin

If we live in a righteous way
We shall be rewarded one day
For those who live in sin today
Truly without God, there is no way!

If You Go

If you go to a football game,
You can't get in the gate;
If you go to a basketball game,
You'll have to wait.

If you go to a card game,
You have to reserve space;
If you go to a beer joint,
You can't get in the place.

If you go to a baseball game,
The bleachers are stacked;
If you go to a dance,
The place is packed.

If you go up on 25 and J,
The devil will be around;
If you go to a movie,
You can't sit down.

If you go to the racetrack,
You can't find a seat to sit down;
If you go to the beach,
You never saw so many people around.

If you go to the carnival,
So many people step on your feet;
You have to wait a long time,
Just to get something to eat.

If you go to a party,
There might not be any ice;
But when it comes to drinking,
Someone will find some spice.

If you go to a party,
You'll do the twist with a grin;
But when you leave this old world,
You can't twist your way in.

If you go to a party,
You might do the stroll;
But what you had better do,
Is to save your soul.

If you go to a party,
You may rock and roll in the groove;
But when God gets ready,
You got to move!

But if you go to church,
What do you see?
Just a few folks here,
Trying to serve Thee.

If you go to church,
What do you find?
Only a few people
Know the value of time.

If you go to church,
What do you hear?
Some servant of God,
Preaching God is near.

If you go to church,
What do you behold?
God is calling wanderers,
Back to the fold.

If you go to church,
What do you perceive?
All things are possible,
If you only believe.

If you go to church,
What do you feel?
Deep down within your soul,
God is real.

If you go to church,
What do you smell?
The Love of God is something,
That everyone must tell.

If you go to church,
What do you taste?
He's calling sinners to repentance,
You have no time to waste.

If you go to church,
What do you do?
Do you take the sermon in?
Or do you sit and chew.

If you go to church,
Do you steal away?
In the midst of the service to prepare
Your soul for that Great Day.

Rev. Ernest L. Hamlin

Sin

This is the world where iniquities persist,
And righteousness often does not exist.
This is the world where personal satisfaction is living,
These characters know no higher Being.

These persons live at the bottom of the net,
Not for what they can give, but what they can get.
Every day they live sublime,
They have not learned the value of time.

Why do these people sin?
Because they know not God within.
Why do these people live as they do?
They have not learned that God is true.

They have not learned that God is right
They live in sin day and night.
They have not given the ultimate in life,
And so they beat upon their wife.

Why must man live in misery?
Why must man live devilishly?
Because man will not give up within,
And this is why man will sin.

Man will not forsake the world,
Man will always seek the golden curl,
Man will never learn to wait,
Because Satan is standing at his gate.

Satan is calling and Satan is getting
While the whole world is fretting
Satan is counting his army anew,
Watch out, brother, he might get you!

Satan does not care how long,
As long as he can sing his song:
"I May Be Late in Getting Through,
But Sooner or Later I'll Get You."

These people live at the liquor store,
Spend and spend until they have no more.
Drunk and disorderly all through the day,
They have just wasted another week's pay.

Little children at home crying
Poor mother is nearly dying;
While daddy's running around town,
With every woman that can be found.

Left-lonesome children, heart-broken wife
God has this sinner's life
It will just be a matter of a day,
For God shall take this sinner's life away.

These are they that have stayed astray,
They really know not night from day;
Useless are the paths they have trod
For they know not the illimitable God.

Oh, they come from both far and near,
But the Gospel, they will not hear;
Rock and roll, calypso and jazz too,
Oh God, they will not listen to you.

These people come and these people go
Bad seeds everywhere do they sow;
They gossip, they lie, they cheat and steal,
They do not know that God is real.

They instigate and they premeditate,
Murder, arson, larceny, and rape.
My friends, crime does not pay,
Oh, if just one of them would find Christ today!

Sin don't always have to be
From sin you can become free
If you would just reach out today
Reach out in your own small way.

Reach out and say, "Lord forgive
Me for the life that I live.
Now anoint my head with oil,
Save me, Lord, lest I fall."

Out of the clutches of the devil,
Save me from the world of evil.
I have sinned and I am a sham
Lord, take me as I am.

Wash me with hyssop,
"Thy name shall I worship"
Wash me clean as I grow
Lord, guide me wherever I go.

Lord, I have lived my life in vain,
Lord let me ride the Glory Train
Up the Golden Streets on high,
Lord, save me before I die.

Lord, I am going, sinking fast,
Lord, save me at last.
Lord, save me on this very day,
For I am softly fading away—away—away.

Rev. Ernest L. Hamlin

That's What God Is to Me

What is God to you?
Without Him what could you do?
He's a ship on a stormy sea
That's what God is to me.

He's Savior to those who are lost
The Comforter who died on Calvary's rugged cross
Jesus Christ yesterday, today, and forever
Turn from Him—No! Never, never.

He's bread when I'm hungry
He's water when I'm thirsty
He's my eyes to see
That's what God is to me.

A mighty fortress is over God
Created He man from dusty sod
The true source of all human power
In God we find a strong tower.

He's my mind, body, and soul
He's so wonderful to behold
He is God Almighty
That's what God is to me.

He's a bridge in deep water
Out in the open, He's a shelter
He's the sunshine, He's the moonlight
I know God will make everything all right.

He's a mother when you're motherless
He's a friend when you're friendless
A source of inspiration and ever-present company
That's what God is to me.

Rev. Ernest L. Hamlin

Let God Come In

I am Alpha and Omega
The Beginning and the End
If you would live free from sin
Then let God come in.

God is not some distant star,
God is not very far
But if you would only begin
To let God come in.

Last night I saw your star,
And realized how near you are
And that's when I began to begin,
Won't you let God come in.

I am not a perfect man
I try to be the best I can
But sometimes I cry from within
Let the church say Amen.

God is my only hope,
In this world I grope;
Try to live as a friend,
But only if you let God come in.

How great Thou art,
My starter and my start,
My friend unto the end
Let God come in.

The Omnipotent Power
With Thy love on me shower
Fill me without and fill me within,
But just let God come in.

O divine Master, grant that I may be
Eternally forever inclined on Thee
I know no remedy for sin
Unless I let God come in.

Out of confusion and despair
The Almighty God is everywhere;
I am not strong enough to make it to the end
That's why I let God come in.

Thank you for the sun that will shine
Thank you for your spirit divine
But I want to see you in the end
The greatest reason I know, to let God come in.

Rev. Ernest L. Hamlin

The Greatest of Them All

Kings rise and kings fall,
But who is the greatest of them all?

Mirror, mirror on the wall,
Who is the greatest of them all?
Mirror, though I am not great at all,
Tell me what is written on the wall.

Mirror, mirror on the wall,
Is he short or is he tall?
Is he large or is he small?
Mirror, mirror on the wall.

Is he strong or is he weak?
Is he haughty or is he meek?
Mirror, mirror on the wall,
Who is the greatest of them all?

Is he shy or is he loud?
Is he modest or is he proud?
Is he unjust or is he fair?
Is he the greatest everywhere?

Is he considerate, caring, and mild?
Is he gentle as a child?
Is he very nice and kind?
Can I be sure he's truly mine?

Mirror, mirror on the wall,
Pride goeth before the fall;
Still I listen for the Call,
Is he Master of us all?

Is he truly the One and only?
Does he love the poor and lonely?
This is a question asked by us all.
Answer me, mirror, mirror on the wall.

Mirror, mirror on the wall,
Is the world moving at all?
If so, what makes it go?
Because He hath made it so.

Who is He that I speak about?
He makes me run, jump, and shout.
And so I ask you, mirror on the wall,
Who is the greatest of them all?

He is He that is He!
He is He that means so much to me.
And so, mirror, mirror on the wall, Tell us,
Who is the greatest of them all? King Jesus...King Jesus...King Jesus.

Rev. Ernest L. Hamlin

Let the Church Be

Let the church be
Let the church be what it is to me
Let the church be free
Let the church be what it is to me.

Let the church be the haven of the free
Let the church be what it must be
Let the church be filled with Thee
Let the church be what it used to be.

Let the church be what it has yet to be
Let the church be the haven of the free
Let the church be as strong as the sea
Let the church be as upright as a tree.

Let the church be as pure as gold
For the half has never been told
Way up in the sky, up above,
Is the dearest One that I love.

Although He is a mystery
Yet, He satisfies me
For way up, way up high,
There's someone bigger than you and I.

I sing because He saved me
Out of nowhere, I met Thee
More powerful than all the elements of the earth could ever be
God placed His hand on me.

The souls that have been saved are many,
But unless in God we trust, We're lost just like this penny.
When one has lived in sin until he's old,
Then what shall he give in exchange for his soul?

Let the church spread the gospel far and near
So that all the sinners will hear
Let the church spread the gospel high and wide
Open the doors! Let the sinners inside.

Good news! Jesus is coming!
Right now; I can hear the angels humming
Up there we won't need any money
We shall feast on milk and honey.

And so, and so, let the church be mighty
Let the church live in the hearts of men eternally
Let the church be the very best there is to be
In service to God and humanity.

Rev. Ernest L. Hamlin

If You Are

You think because you are a Christian,
You're too good to speak to the sinner down the street;
You think you're too good to talk
To the drunkards that you meet.

But if you are a real Christian,
Humble yourself at Jesus' feet;
Do whatever you can
For whomever you meet.

You think because you are Christian,
You have to get to church on time;
You don't have time to stop,
To give some poor soul a dime.

But if you are a real Christian,
Humble yourself at Jesus' feet;
Do whatever you can
For whomever you meet.

You think because you are a Christian,
You don't have time anymore;
To associate with your old friends,
And so you leave them standing at your door.

But if you are a real Christian,
Humble yourself at Jesus' feet;
Do whatever you can,
For whomever you meet.

You think because you are a Christian,
You don't have time you feel;
To deal with bums and tramps,
When they ask you for a meal.

But if you are a real Christian,
Humble yourself at Jesus' feet;
Do whatever you can,
For whomever you meet,

You think because you are a Christian,
You can choose with whom to associate;
But old Satan is waiting for you,
Standing firm at old Hell's gate.

But if you are a real Christian,
Humble yourself at Jesus' feet;
Do whatever you can,
For whomever you meet.

Rev. Ernest L. Hamlin

This Man

Almost two thousand years ago;

A man was born and a man died
A man suffered and the world cried
But this was not an ordinary man
This man was part of an Infinite Plan.

This man gave all that He could give
He was the strangest man who ever lived
Healing the sick and raising the dead
Men came to Him lying on their bed.

Not a one of them did He turn away
This man taught us how to pray
People came from far and near
For the Gospel, they wanted to hear.

For the teachings that He taught
For the guidance that they sought
For the ends of being and ideal grace
They wanted to see the Master's face.

Men came to Him lame
Men came to Him in shame
But when they left, they could walk
And when they left, they began to talk.

They talked about the lonely Jesus
They talked about how He saved us.
I just stopped by to tell you
What God can do for you.

What He has done for others
He'll do for you, sisters and brothers;
For I am convinced beyond a shadow of doubt,
Whatever the situation, God will bring you out.

This man came and this man went
Saving mankind, His life was spent
Not for some personal gain,
But, to get man on board the "Glory Train."

Kingdoms come, rise and fall,
But this man was the strangest of them all.
Why should I, the enemy, fear
When I know that this man is near.

Two thousand years ago and yet;
He lives as no other man I have met;
For out of sin, I was made free,
I'm so glad today that this man found me.

Rev. Ernest L. Hamlin

If Any Man

If any man suffer as a Christian
Let him not be ashamed
If any man suffer as a Christian
Let him not seek fame.

If any man suffer as Christian
Let him suffer in My name
If any man suffer as a Christian
Let him not be ashamed.

If any man suffer as a Christian
Let not his sufferings be in vain
If any man suffer as a Christian
Let him not be ashamed.

If any man suffer as a Christian
From sin let him refrain
If any man suffer as a Christian
Let him not be ashamed.

If any man suffer as a Christian
Let him come in from the rain
For sin beats upon him
As rodents upon the harvest of grain.

Yet if any man will humble himself
Let him not be ashamed
They came, they sought, they found
The blind, the crippled, the lame.

Christ gave His blood and body
From sin you can refrain
For Jesus said: "This do ye
Until I come again."

If any man denies himself
His life shall not be in vain
If any man will but serve Christ
The Tree of Life shall be his gain.

If any man will ride
Let him ride the Glory Train
If any man will sing
Let him sing the Hallelujah refrain.

If any man suffer as a Christian
Let him not seek fame
If any man suffer as a Christian
Let him not be ashamed.

Rev. Ernest L. Hamlin

If I Had My Way

If I had it my way
What would the world say?
Would it be just another day?
Would it be sad or would it be gay?

If I had my way
These are the words that I would say:
Lord, help me this very day
To help some sinner along the way.

If I had my way
What could I do or say?
Lord, help me to really be
Of some humble service to Thee.

If I had my way
I would kneel down and pray
Lord, send me, for here am I
And for Thee I shall gladly die.

If I had my way
People would be happy to say
Good morning to a friend
And thankful to see the day begin.

If I had my way
I would be content each day
Just to feel His precious Love
Because it's sent down from Heaven above.

If I had my way
There would be no more fighting
If men could only learn today
That doing God's Will is delighting.

If I had my way
There would be no more gambling
If men would stop going astray
Then they should stop rambling.

If I had my way
There would be no more cheating
If every man could find each day
A day that is worth repeating.

If I had my way
There would be no more stealing
For night would be as bright as day
And the Holy Spirit would be revealing.

If I had my way
There would be no more cursing
For mankind would long each day
For the Songs of Zion to sing.

If I had my way
There would be no more killing
Each soul would pray
And give the uttermost shilling.

If I had my way
There would be no more drinking
For each day along the way
On Jesus, men would be thinking.

If I had my way
There would be no time for smoking
For we must make a call each day
For the telephone in our bosom must ring.

If I had my way
There would be no more lying
Every soul would shout and pray
There would be no time for sighing.

If I had my way
There would be no more sin
For not only this day, but everyday
With every beat of my heart, God dwells within.

There Is a Need

There is a need for men
Who would blaze the unknown trail.
There is a cure for sin
If Jesus, men would hail.

There is a need for love
The unconquerable virtue
For there is a God above
A God that's so true.

There is a need for kindness
If we would only show;
For the road to true success
Comes only if God we know.

There is a need for charity
The love of all mankind
There is a need for honesty
To the Savior so divine.

There is a need for peace
When will the struggle end?
When will the torment cease?
Is it just around the bend?

There is a need for God
For man has strayed away
There is a road that we have not trod
There is a way today.

There is need for Jesus
The Savior of us all
For if He is to lead us
We must harken to His call.

There is a need today
For the sinner to repent
Give ye an account some way
Of the life on earth you spent.

There is a need for brotherhood
If men would walk together today
Each man would be understood
For the true answer is to learn to pray.

There is a need for the whole world to get down on its knees
And pray to God Almighty today
There is a need for our countless pleas
Asking God Almighty to show us the way.

A True Mother and Christ

A true mother will stick by you
Through thick and thin, my friend
It's not what you did or do
A true mother will see you through.

But Jesus Christ is more than a mother
He'll stick to you closer than a brother
The most potent force in anyone's life
That force, my friend, is Jesus Christ.

Rev. Ernest L. Hamlin

God Is Not Dead

Some people are so foolish
And some are so childish
Some people will say anything
And some will believe anything.

You can't make me doubt Him
Because I know too much about Him
I don't care what I read
I know that God is not dead.

"Walk By Faith, Not Sight"

II Corinthians 5:1–7

Walk by faith, not sight,
It isn't by luck that we win or lose
Pattern your life after Jesus Christ
You may serve Him if you choose.

If you serve Him the times will be hard,
Sometimes things will get tough
But don't sink, just wait on God,
For Christianity is made of sterner stuff.

Though the trials that beset you are great,
Though the toils you endure are many,
God will answer prayer if you but wait
And His blessings upon you shall be plenty.

When we walk by faith, we walk in the light
When we walk by sight, we walk in the dark,
Through faith we walk in the path of right
With sight the Comforter leaves no mark.

If you cannot sing like angels,
If you cannot preach like Paul,
You can tell the Love of Jesus,
And say He died for all.

Without Him, circumstances upset us
Without Him sometimes we worry
Walk by faith, and in Him we trust
Walk in the light of His glory.

Walk by faith as the apostles did,
Being beaten for God is no shame
To them the gospel could not be hid
They rejoiced to suffer shame for His name.

If your work be of men
Then it will come to naught,
But is it because of God—Amen
Then it shall be eternally sought.

Fight the good fight of faith forever
Live as if you had to meet Jesus today
Your love for the Savior never sever
You will receive your crown someday.

I Thought I Knew

I thought I knew you
I thought I knew what to do
I thought that I could see
As far as the ocean or tree.

I thought that I had found the way
To end the stress and strain of never-ending day,
I thought that I had come to the end,
But now I realize that I must begin.

I must begin now the work of my Father
I must serve Him and no other
For when I gave my life to Him
The world seemed lonesome and grim.

But now I see the mystery of His work
And I must never try to shirk
I walk down a lonely road,
On my back I carry a heavy load.

But I cannot stray from the path
For the way is more certain pi in math
God knows what is best for us all
I must answer my Father's call.

I thought I knew when day was done
But my work has yet to be begun
I must press forward through the heat and cold
Onward my God to save my soul.

There are times when the way seems hard
Yet I press forward to see my God
Though my enemies encamp round about me
Yet will I trust eternally in Thee.

I thought I knew beauty
Something that's as pure as sap from a tree
But this one thing has been revealed to me
I have not found love and sincerity.

I thought I knew the right one
The one upon which there would be no setting sun
But I must go further up the road to see
If there is anyone for me

I thought I knew love
But love comes only from above
For love was not put in your heart to stay
Love is only love when you give it way.

What Have We Got to Lose?

II Kings 7:1–4

If we go to the city
On us, Lord, have pity
For there is a famine there
We can get food nowhere!

If we go, we shall die there
Which is no better than dying here
For death is but death
Death is the cessation of breath.

If we sit here, there is no cheer
For as certain as we sit here
The inevitability of death is near
So why sit we here?

If we fall unto the Syrian host
The certainty of death is foremost
But perhaps they will let us be
Come, let us go and see.

If we never venture to go
Then surely we will never know
But if we dare to go and inquire
Perhaps we shall rise out of this mire.

God told Abraham, "Offer your son for a burnt offering,"
Abraham did not ask God for any explaining
He knew he had to do
What God told him to do.

God told Jonah to Nineveh go
But Jonah did his own thing, you know
Jonah boarded a ship for Tarshish at Joppa
But when God gets ready He'll stop ya.

They threw Daniel in the lion's den
Old Daniel said, "Bring on the lions, men
I want you all to see this day
How the Lord will make a way."

Young Joseph was sold into slavery
Later he was incarcerated because of his loyalty
But he was brought forth one day
He was made a ruler in a big way.

We find little David playing a harp
You know man of God cannot be stopped
When David fought Goliath, the odds were great
But David knew God is the designer of fate.

Job was made Exhibit A in faithfulness
Despite all of his vicissitudes and distress
Job clung to the faith and hung on
After a while trial was over and victory was won.

So whatever we choose
What have we got to lose?

Good For Nothing

Jeremiah the Lord said, "A linen girdle go and get
Put it around your waist and don't get it wet."
Strange words coming from the Lord of all
We must obey His requests lest we fall.

So Jeremiah did as the Lord told him to
He did not know what he had to do
But Jeremiah knew as a child of the King
That he must be willing to do anything.

And so God spoke to Jeremiah again
And the words of God were very plain
Jeremiah a linen girdle go and get
Put it around your waist and don't get it wet.

God called Jeremiah and he obeyed the call
For Jeremiah was man who stood tall
Though it was indeed an odd request
The words of God Jeremiah did not contest.

Jeremiah took the girdle and hid it away
After some time the Lord said, "Go get it today."
Down by the Euphrates, there it was hid
The Lord said go, and Jeremiah did.

When it was dug up, it did reveal
A message, it did not conceal
Behold the girdle that was something
Had become good for nothing!

"Jeremiah," said the Lord, "I've got some people in Judah and Jerusalem
Who pursue not Godly things, for the things that are evil fascinate them
I will mar their pride
Oh yes! From God you cannot hide"

These evil people God's words refuse to hear
For the flowery words of the world were more endearing to the ear.
On the highway of life God's words point the way
And those who refuse to listen must pay the price one day.

This group was walking after other gods,
And so it was time for the chastening rod
They were serving and worshipping other gods, you see
But God said, "Thou shall have no other gods before Me."

As this girdle is, which used to be something,
But now is good for nothing,
So shall this evil people be
Who refuse to serve Me.

When the Savior Comes

You might be feeling low
But you'll get up and go
When the Savior comes.

You might be feeling down and out
But you'll jump and shout
When the Savior comes.

It might be at night
He'll make everything all right
When the Savior comes.

It might be in the day
He'll help you along your way
When the Savior comes.

You might be friendless
You'll surely be blessed
When the Savior comes.

You might be almost gone
He'll take you on home
When the Savior comes.

You might be standing in the door
There's room for one more
When the Savior comes.

You might be on your bed
He'll put you ahead
When the Savior comes.

We shall sing
Joy bells will ring
When the Savior comes.

You might be on the ground
You'll surely be found
When the Savior comes.

Heaven will rejoice
For those who have made the right choice
When the Savior comes.

In sin you may abound
He'll turn you around
When the Savior comes.

You might be alone
The way to you will be shown
When the Savior comes.

You might begin to cry
Jesus will wipe your eye
When the Savior comes.

The Meaning of Sunday School

S - is for the Sabbath Day
U - is for unity along the way
N - is for nothing that is less
D - means duty that is best
A - is for activity that is done
Y - is for youth that have been won.

S - is for the Savior of the fold
C - is for the cross that saves the soul
H - is for heaven, the home of us all
O - is for the opportunity to heed the call
O - is for openness of heart, the willingness to shout
L - is for the Love of God, that's what Sunday School is all about.

This poem was written in commemoration of the Year of Jubilee (60) of the Good Shepherd Baptist Church, Richmond, Virginia. The poem was written as a personal tribute to the work of Good Shepherd Church and shared at the Jubilee Banquet on June 3, 1978.
Rev. Dr. Paul Nichols was Senior Minister.

Rev. Ernest L. Hamlin

Sixty Years

In 1918 in the year of Lord
A group of Christians got together on one accord
They founded a church, so it did seem
It was the beginning of a sixty-year dream.

Good Shepherd Baptist was its name
Robert C. Williams was the engineer on the train
He served the congregation well, so I'm told
Many converts did he add to the fold.

Andrew D. Smith was the second man on board
He used to raise the roof singing many a chord
For thirty-two years, he led his members here
And the congregation still holds his memory dear.

In 1960 Paul Nichols became head man number three
He came here all the way from Bowling Green, Kentucky
He couldn't sing like angels, but he could preach like Paul
He told the Love of Jesus who died for us all.

Sixty years is a long time for only three
Ministers to serve a congregation the size of thee
The attrition rate at some churches is so high
It seems the ministers, a revolving door go by.

For sixty years the congregation has stood the test of time
Souls have been saved, there has been enlightenment of the mind
The church is full every Sunday morning I see
This is the way God's church ought to be.

There is a place for everyone to be
There's deacons and ushers and even a nursery
There's the story hour and choir you know
There's the youth fellowship, men's fellowship, and more to go.

There's the Family Night Dinner and lots of fun
The Field Day Event where the kids jump and run
There's the Senior Citizens and of course Sunday School you know
There's the Clothes Closet and even more to go.

There's Boy Scouts, Cub Scouts, and Girl Scouts too
There is always something for everybody to do.
So don't sit back and wait to be asked
Find your place and set about doing the task.

There's deaconesses all dressed in white
The prayer meeting and teacher's meeting on Wednesday night
There's baptismal classes as you might well guess
There's the men's chorus, but the one that I like best

Is the children's choir, don't ask me why
For it is the children who will carry on after we die
I like to see the children on Children's Day
They need a chance to put their talents on display.

Good Shepherd Baptist Church, I salute you
Sixty years of work, that was well done too
Don't rest on your laurels, there is more work to do
Saving souls is work that is done by too few.

S - is for the souls that have been saved
I - is for the intensity the way has been paved
X - is the symbol of Christ and His Love
T - is for the talent that God has given from above
Y - is for the youth of the church today
      the builders of tomorrow's church in every way.

Y - is for the years that over our heads have rolled
E - is for the eagerness that has been unfold
A - is for the anticipation of what the future will hold
R - is for the righteousness that never grows old
S - is for the Shepherd who heads the flock
      The Savior who opens the door for those who knock.

If We Love God

Whatever the cross may be,
The Love of God can set us free.
Whatever the burden's weight,
The Love of God can liberate.

Whatever problems may fall,
God Loves us one and all.

When the trials never seem to cease,
Just look to God and He will give you peace.

When enemies press you down on every hand,
Just look to God and take your stand.

When troubles come in the midnight hour,
God will supply your strength and power.

When you just don't know what to do,
Look to God and He will see you through.

IF WE LOVE GOD, THE LOVE OF GOD
LIBERATES US FROM THE CROSSES IN OUR LIVES.

When you've tried everything there is to try,
Why don't you give God a try?

Whenever you start to cry,
God will wipe your face dry.

When your friends leave you,
God will not deceive you.

When your family is dead and gone,
God will never leave you alone.

When you're on your bed of affliction,
God will raise you up with no restriction.

When you're down and out,
God will bring you out.

When you're lost and can't find your way,
God will pick you up and show you the way.

IF WE LOVE GOD, THE LOVE OF GOD
LIBERATES US FROM THE CROSSES IN OUR LIVES.

If we have tried and just can't make it,
Satan's chains, we don't have to take it.

The arms of God can make us free,
They stand waiting for you and me.

The Gospel Train is rolling every day,
Won't you step on board and take your stay.

Jesus is the conductor, the ticket taker,
He makes the assignments to see the Maker.

God is the engineer on this train,
The way is so simple and so plain.

Open your heart to Jesus and repent,
When Jesus said, "Come," this is what He meant:
There can be no rest for you and me,
Until our souls rest in the arms of Thee.

IF WE LOVE GOD, THE LOVE OF GOD
LIBERATES US FROM THE CROSSES IN OUR LIVES.

Rev. Ernest L. Hamlin

"What Kind of Seeds Are We Sowing"

Mark 4:1–8

To err is human, to forgive is divine
As we daily live, on marches Time.
Let us not be in err, when we should be knowing
I wonder, what kind of seeds are we sowing?

When the sun rises on the eastern horizon
And another day has arisen and is done
What have our labors and aspirations been this day?
Have we truly lived in a just and righteous way?

When the sun fades behind the western hill
Do we have peace in our souls still?
Or has the day brought tragedy and despair?
Are we moving forward in life or going nowhere?

When the moon rises and it is night
Are we able to see what is right?
Or are we just trying to make a good showing?

When the stars spangle the air
And we perceive the beauty up there
As we gaze upon the moonlit sky
And ask ourselves how, when, where, and why?

Are we living as God would have us live?
Not for what we can get, but what we can give
Are we each day spiritually growing?
What kind of seeds are we really sowing?

Have we gone out to sow or merely reap?
Have we gone out to give or merely keep?
Have we tried to be the best in our every endeavor?
Or have we tried to deceive, disrupt, and sever?

Have we sown seeds by the wayside?
Because we went out with a lot of pride
Then the birds of the air came and swooped it up
To sow in vain is to drink from the bitter cup.

Have we sown seeds upon stony ground?
Where not much earth could be found
Immediately will it spring up, so we see
But it cannot stand the forces of adversity.

For when the noonday sun begins to shine
It becomes scorched and is no longer thine
Because it is not grounded deep into the earth
It withers away, it dies soon after birth.

Have we sown among the thorns somewhere?
We did not see them, but they were there

And when they grew up, to the seeds they did apply
And henceforth no fruit did the seeds supply.

Have we sown seeds upon fertile ground?
Where good fruit grows and can be found?
It increases, it expands, it multiplies, so I'm told
Some thirty, some sixty, and some a hundred fold.

I pray that all our seeds may be upon fertile ground
If we want to see the Master, this is where we must be found,
We must not be in err, we must beknowing,
It is the right kind of seeds that we must be sowing.

Rev. Ernest L. Hamlin

"A Follower or a Hollerer"

John 11:37–44

They say we can't do this
We can't do that
But you go ahead and lead
And we'll follow.

They say we've been doing this for years
Ain't no need to change now
As he begins to lead,
They begin to holler.

The difference between a follower and a hollerer is this:
A follower keeps an open mind
And a hollerer keeps an open mouth
The difference is even more acute.

A follower knows when to speak out,
But all the time his mind is still open,
A hollerer is always speaking out
But his mind is never open.

A lot of times people will say
The pastor wants the church to put on a program
I'm not supporting it because
I don't like the chairperson of the committee.

We ain't got time for this kind of foolishness
God's house is a house of Love
And if we can't get together on one accord
We had better get on our knees and ask the Lord,

For more guidance, more patience, and more love
We ain't got time for dissension and hate
If we are doing what we're supposed to do,
Then God will surely see us through.

If you don't like the way a person is doing the job
Then go to him or her and lend a helping hand
For the time will surely come when we too
Will need some help in what we seek to do.

If God is our Father and Jesus is our Friend
Then let us begin again and be what we must be
If the Gospel is to be lived upon the earth
It must be lived in us.

Remember the words of our Lord and Master
Whenever we find ourselves getting in someone's way
Don't stand between someone and God, and so
Remember Jesus said, "Unbind him and let him go!"

Rev. Ernest L. Hamlin

"God Told Jonah to Go to Ninevah"

Jonah 1:1–17

Nineveh is significant because it was a notorious town
Everywhere you went sin did abound
In every section of the city
Satan reigned. It was such a pity.

On every street, on every road,
Satan carried a heavy load.
Not since Sodom and Gomorrah had there been such a wicked place,
Satan made himself manifest in every face.

Then in the early morn,
Satan's activities were born
Sin had no special time to begin,
You just sin and then sin again.

Verily Jesus says to you,
I send a voice to lead you,
Into the paths of repentance,
He will guide you.

Even as I am known,
So shall you be known
Behold I am the Way
The Day of Salvation is today.

Heaven's Gates stand ready,
To receive you who are astray
Turn to Him and be forgiven,
Come to Him today.

You can run from the sun,
You can run from the moon
You can run all night and all day,
But from God you can't run away!

Rev. Ernest L. Hamlin

"When The Prodigal Son Returns Home"

Luke 15:11–24

What will you do?
When the Prodigal Son returns home
What will you say?
When the Prodigal Son returns your way.

Will you be kind?
As the loving father was
Or will you be indifferent and cold?
Like the older brother, so we're told.

When the Prodigal Son returns home
From a distant and faraway place
Will you greet him with a frown?
Or a smile on your face.

When the Prodigal Son returns home
After wasting his substance in riotous living
Will you be cynical and snide?
Or will you be loving and forgiving.

I tell you the Prodigal Son has returned home
You see him in the marketplace, on the street
The Prodigal Son is everyone you meet
The high, the low, the in between, the indiscreet.

The Prodigal Son is anyone and everyone
Everyone who has gone away.
Everyone who has gone astray
Everyone who has fallen by the way.

The Prodigal Son lives and moves and has his being
In the lives of all of those who have done
Something that was not right
Something that was seen in a bad light.

People do wrong things and people will make a mistake
But thanks be to the Father who gives us a break
In as much as the Father forgives us of our wrong
So should we forgive others, all the day long.

All of God's children should rejoice
All of God's children should raise their voice
Hallelujah! Praise the Lord! Never more to roam!
When the Prodigal Son returns home.

Rev. Ernest L. Hamlin

Your Life in Christ

Does your life in Christ make you an example for another?
Or is it really a bother?
If you are ashamed to own Him
He'll be ashamed to own you before the Father.

Does your life shine before others?
Then why run when you can help your brothers?
Just a little help you can do it
Jesus outrates all others.

Do you live for what you can get?
Not caring how you get what you get
Trying to walk in the rain and not get wet
Why not try Jesus's umbrella, it's the best yet.

No rain, no snow will ever fall on you
Jesus's umbrella is big enough for me and you
All you have to do is reach out and get
The best person protection yet.

Has Jesus changed your life?
Taken out all the stress and strife
Then you're under the Master's plan
Welcome, lost sheep, to the fold again.

"The Superiority of Divinity Over Humanity"

Matthew 26:36–46

Jesus said, Stay ye here a little while,
While I go over yonder to pray.
When He got back, the disciples were asleep
It's the same way today.

Everyone wants to be in the group
But no one wants to pay the price
A disciple must not fall asleep on the job,
The disciples did it thrice.

The first time you say, anybody can make a mistake
The second time it was a bad time of day
The third time, it didn't make any difference,
Because Jesus had already made a way out of no way.

The spirit is willing, but the flesh is weak
That's why we can't put our trust in earthly man
In order to find peace and serenity
We must put our trust in the Eternal Man.

God was, is, and ever shall be
The source of all strength and power
In Him, we find the Way
He is a bridge and a mighty tower.

Man will turn his back on man, but Jesus never fails
Man's attitude changes like the seasons
Man will stand you up and put you down
Man sometimes won't even tell you his reasons.

The disciples forsook Jesus, but Jesus has never forsaken His disciples,
He was there in the Upper Room with His men
He was in the burning bush on the backside of the mountain
And He's coming back to receive His kin.

Man's nature is changeable, but Jesus is with you always
Man will be with you when you're up, and without you when you're down
But Jesus will be with you when you're up,
Semi up, semi down, down, and all the way round.

Divinity is superior over humanity because
Divinity understands humanity, while humanity does not understand itself.
We don't know why we do some of the things we do.
God understands and He manifested that understanding through His Son, Jesus
I don't understand everything and neither do you.

Jesus is the consolidation of divinity and humanity rolled into one
Humanity had erred and gone astray
Divinity was necessary to undo what was done
So Jesus came our way to show us the Way.

Divinity is superior over humanity because humanity could not get the job done
Whenever one agent fails to do the job, God always has another.
Man is prone to error, to err is human,
A Christian must always help his brother.

Humanity is seeking real peace
Divinity is the true answer we seek
We can open our mouths,
But only God enables us to speak.

We can open our eyes,
But only God enables us to see.
We can open our minds,
But only God enables us to be.

We can open our hearts,
But only God enables us to love
The Love of God reaches out to one another
And reaches from down here to up above.

Rev. Ernest L. Hamlin

The Liar

Every time you see a liar on the street
The first thing he does is show his teeth
The next thing, he'll tell a lie
You had better let that liar pass on by.

You see him running all over town
He's forever spreading lies around
Every time he opens his mouth
He lies north, east, west, and south.

Liar, why don't you stop lying?
Tell the truth, you better start trying
One day you'll have to account for every lie
Before the Judgement Hall of God in the sweat by and by.

Liar, why can't you be sincere?
Regardless to whether I'm near
Why do you treat me so mean?
Just because I'm not on the scene.

Every time you open your mouth, you tell a lie
If you didn't lie your mouth would be dry
Lying seems to quench your thirst
So you drink later and lie first.

Liar, oh liar, why do you lie so much?
Always bearing false witness and such
Deceiving is your middle name
Because deception is your claim to fame.

Liar, oh liar, you can do no right
I wish you would get out of sight
Liar, oh liar, all you do is wrong
You're just as wrong as the day is long.

Tell the truth, you just won't do
I guess because it's just not in you
But you'll tell a lie in a wink
You love to lie as a drunk loves to drink.

You can't depend on him for a favor
With his mouth, he'll destroy his neighbor
He gives lip service wherever he does go
A tight lip is something he does not know.

You profess to be a Christian
But you don't know how to listen
How can you or I be a Christian? If we
Just keep on lying from here to eternity.

Rev. Ernest L. Hamlin

"The Legacy of the Cross"

Matthew 16:24–28

What can the legacy of the Cross be?
C - is for Christ who set us free
R - is for righteousness you can see
O - is for only God is real to me
S - is for suffering on Calvary
S - is for servant of humanity

The legacy of the Cross is threefold
It's physical, psychological, and spiritual
It's an upright post with a cross piece near the top
It's a trial or affliction that never seems to stop.

It's a symbol known the world over
It's the object on which Jesus was crucified
In Pilate's hall, Jesus was tried
On Calvary's Cross, He hung, bled, and died.

It's what's handed down to us
From ancestor, predecessor, or from the past
The world is moving at a rate that's fast
Only what we do for Christ will last.

He said to the water, "Peace, be still!"
The waters no more did rock and reel.
O ye of little faith, said He
Understandest thou not the power of divinity.

It is the capability of manifested power
It is the constant prayer of every hour
It is the constant knowledge that God is near
He takes away our every fear.

It is the humility of every saved soul
Those who affirmed the gospel story of old
Every knee must bow and every tongue confess
Jesus is Lord! Salvation is best!

It is the love of man for his fellow man
It is the love of God's eternal plan
It is the kind of love that you can feel
It is the kind of love that is real.

What can the legacy of the Cross be?
It is the best in service to humanity
Man fell and he was lost
For him Jesus died, This is the legacy of the Cross!

Rev. Ernest L. Hamlin

Prayer

P - is for the patience that He has taught us
R - is for the radiance His Spirit has brought us
A - is for the ability He gives to us
Y - is for the youth that lives through us
E - is for the energy He bestows upon us
R - is for the righteousness that grows upon us

Put them all together and what have you got?
P-R-A-Y-E-R, a word to us that means a lot.

Whether I Live or Die

If one can give, Then one can live
But all must die, As well as you and I

If I must live by a shot in the back,
Then let me die pressed to the wall, but fighting back.
For if I but live in fear,
Then I shall but die in fear.

But let me live in courage spreading God's marvelous light,
Let me die as a man who was a valiant knight.
Let me die by God's shining sea,
Knowing just how I have served Thee.

Let me die with the sword in my hand,
Fighting for God, here I stand:
Not as a boy with a toy,
But as a man full of joy.

Let me die by the stormy banks
Giving God my humble thanks;
Not dying as a coward or a fool,
But making my enemies my footstool.

Let me die on the silver shore
Loving God forevermore
Not because I'm dying now,
But because I shall wear a starry crown.

Let me die,
So that I,
Can forever be,
In the land of the free.

Let me die on the highway of life,
Sharing the trouble, toil, and strife;
Not because it's over now,
But on the devil I frown.

Let me die where the race of men go by,
They are sinners, but so am I,
In the light of Thy shining face;
Thank God, we're saved by grace.

Whether I live or die,
I'm going home to the sweet by and by
Never a worry, never a care,
Because Jesus will be there.

Whether it's time or not, I'm ready,
Hold my hand, Lord, keep me steady,
Let me die as the martyrs have died,
Fighting for God because the Glory Train I desire to ride.

"The Eyes of God Are Smiling Down on Me"

Matthew 6:25–34

Man being the finite creature that he is
Is always susceptible to error
That's why we need a Savior
To oversee our every endeavor.

God was, is, and always shall be
The Source to whom we go for every need
He stands willing, ready, and able
To pardon our every evil deed.

He sees all we do, He hears all we say
He even knows our thoughts before we do
Even the hairs upon our head are numbered
God knows what is best for me and you.

His eyes are not bound by limitation
His eyes perceive beyond our imagination
God is the God of love
God is the God of all creation.

From the crack of dawn,
God watches over His family
Until the end of the day
The eyes of God are smiling down on me.

Man stands before the altar of God
Empty, bent, broken, and unworthy
Of God's Love, that He shares with all,
But God supplies it freely to you and me.

Rev. Ernest L. Hamlin

We don't always know what God's will is
We don't always do as He says do
But just as sure as we are living
The eyes of God are smiling down on you.

Sometimes we don't hear the voice of God
Sometimes we only hear the voice of man
But God speaks to us not from far away,
He speaks through us, listen to His plan.

God moves in mysterious ways
And we don't always understand what He says
But if we would only let Him use us
We would be blessed the rest of our days.

Sometimes it seems that nothing works for us
Sometimes doors keep closing in our face
If we would only wait on the Lord,
He'll show us where to go to be in place.

Sometimes we wonder, "Why me, Lord?"
Sometimes everybody is moving and we're still standing still
God has a lesson for us to learn,
When we do, with His Spirit we'll be filled.

I wonder what God's plan is for my life
I have tried to conceive it with my mind
God does not work by man's time frame,
His Will will be revealed in due time.

I have often asked God to give me what I want,
God will not be confined by the mind of man
God will reach out to us
And give us a helping hand.

God will give me what He wants me to have,
He will meet my every earthly need,
All I have to do is trust in Him
My body and soul, He will feed.

Christians, let us unite and be forever true
The eyes of God are smiling down on you
Christians, let us set our spirits free
The eyes of God are smiling down on me.

When daylight fades,
And when the sky is bright,
I'm not afraid though I may walk alone,
I'm not afraid because
I know there is no need to fear
The eyes of God are smiling down on me.